I'm a cephalopod trapped in a bi pedal land dwelling mammals body

Ivy Max

DEDICATION

This book is dedicated to the many amazing souls that inspired it.
Especially Evan Frazier, Jill Pinnt, Andrew Lees, Leah Nicole, Kelly, Josh,
Adam, Scott, Erik, Shane and Nathan Broaddus.

CONTENTS

ACKNOWLEDGMENTS

I would like to acknowledge Murray my fat wiener dog.
Seriously, he is very fat.

Into the Sway

there is a small sway to you
almost a quiver in your shoulders
and a smirk that creeps into your smile
a crease in your chin as you tilt your head
you don't even notice me when I'm present
how could you possibly know me when I'm away?
I was your moment once
now I'm nothing but a side thought
you will never be the one
the one with balls enough to
to pull me away from the past

Battleship

there were too many faults
lay lines left unmonitored
things have a tendency to collapse
menial cracks can tear apart a vessel
these things happen everyday
there was no choice but to rebuild
become something different all together
the choice we have now
I have now
is what to become.
the possibilities are endless

Comic Book Romance

fuck
the world falls apart sometimes
our heroes are reduced to rubble
and we all find ourselves stumbling
this is the starting point
I love you
I'm looking for a new hero
mine have been devastated and broken down
it's a big job
but you have all the qualifications
please inquire within

Glance

the desire to escape is intolerable
it's no longer a need to just leave
I need to unzip
and step out of this skin
find a new me to dwell within
one who's not down trodden with affliction
one who's beauty lies in just a look
I will be the me that leaves you in longing
and I will be that woman
that can carry a crowd's glance on her shoulder
I will be the person I've been waiting to meet

Bedtime Stories

and time hunkers forward
and I'm left with just the scraps
the things that can barely sustain a memory
The more I try to look forward
the more I find myself glancing back at you
there is nothing to say
you were a moment
a beautiful one
constructed of lincoln logs
and cello strings
you are my beauty lost to the beast
you make for such a good story
but happy endings are rare
in this
our real lives
and every time I step into an overturned garden
or an abandoned warehouse
you will be the smell that crosses my mind
you are a moment
one of the best

Scott

your voice brings me home
the doorway is open
and I have seen you in a new light
I apologize for my lack of observance
I didn't realize the dedication
but I have acquired a new understanding
of what was at stake
I'm aware now that I have a small piece of you
in my palm
I will handle it carefully
I will do my best to give you no new wounds
nothing you're forced to heal from
I will love you
I promise to try my hardest
to be what you need

After Thoughts

I can feel the weight
lift from my eyelids
as I allow the words well up
and pass through the toll

I can feel my breath
escape in small bursts
the touch of my hand on my face
when am I going to know?
this is where the road breaks
I have to decide which way
the pull is so great in every direction
I know the answer
you're not part of it
I have to find me
I have so many places to go
I'm finally in a position...
to be there.
this could be it
things are going to change so fast
I think I've earned it

Responsible Abandon

are you aware the shape I'm in?
expectancy
Life expectancy.
This is the expectation of life.
How could anyone know what to expect from life?
shall we shed the expectancy?
Let's just call it life
let's abandon the expectations
every moment can be something new
things look dark and looming now,
but tomorrow
the forecast will change
It's amazing the light you can find in the traveling clouds
every moment
from here to there
will be something worth missing
don't forget to loom
in all the seconds from here until now
and remember...
I will do my best to be there
when you embark on the now.

Eventual Content

I found it
the inspiration I was seeking
it just fell upon me
I was keeping it contained
for fear of tears and, well...snot
but it just showed up
you showed up on my doorstep
you should go home
all that lies here is unfortunate
I will grant you twenty pounds
that is the threshold for forgiveness
in the end
sickness will devour this part of me

Shane

sometimes in those awkward moments of the morning
when all has gone astray
and the rules have been laid to waste
I see you
you encompass everything I want someone to be
your faults only draw me in
I will never be the right one
and I will grow to do this in the most graceful way
but tonight
I just want to pass that moment with you
the one where the love is unrequited
I have the uncanny feeling that you will wake up one day
and understand how I feel
I wish you the best of luck when that moment arises
I know the pain of being unwanted
I would imagine
the pain of being forgotten is much worse

Brett Jason

I will let you be here today
it's been years
and I spend every day in an attempt to live your legacy
but tonight
it's just me missing you
I love you
all of you.....
I couldn't ask for sweeter demons on my shoulder
and Nate
we will take an extra shot for you
I will stay here, behind and carry the torch for all of us
I hope you have all found each other on the other half
your absence keeps me present
you were my presents
thank you

Minions

I swayed alone
no desperation falling forth in any regard
I let myself miss childhood for a moment
and I wandered through adolescence
I found myself struggling through my twenties
making good decisions
and bad
I saw myself become confident
and loving
I saw myself yesterday
and imagined me ten minutes from now
at the end of all that
I found
that I will always be me
and I will always need you
all of you
you are my foundation and soil that I come from
every word exchanged and look shared
is the place I come home to
so this is my wish for every one of you
that today
you will have a moment
to sit down and realize how much you matter
in every regard
this is my birthday wish
thank you for being a part of my life

Forgotten Moments

grace is what brings me home
it's why I lay here now
and why I will leave silent in the morning
my love no longer resides here
I can no longer be yours
or anyone else's
but you will be the person I hope to see again
you will be something I loved
but
I'm done now
you will take someone by surprise
and be everything they needed
you will never be mine
but thank you for the attempt
it's over now

Amira

the sweetest blessing of truth and sincerity
you are the reason people like me look forward to the future
you will be the masses one day
you will be the hope for the rest of us
I see a collective universe in your eyes
may you always be blessed by a world that loves you
may I always be blessed with a world that has you in it

Both Arms

I've lost hope
and my faith is dwindling
I have fallen
my knees and palms are bloody
I can barely lift my head
my mind is sinking
as I fall
and my vision blurs...
I can see you
I can see you in my future
I can tolerate the pain as I push myself to my feet
clarity rains slowly over me
in the midst of a deluge
there is no reason to feign tearlessness

as each lost drop of faith
hits the ground a midst an on pour
I can feel seeds bursting to roots
I can see the wooden foundation build beneath me
a bewilderment of tiny motions
clung to one another
creaking and scraping
sifting the dirt amid the churn
the feel
of something growing
building
I am here
I will tend and own the ground beneath us all
and I will rise up
bountiful and bearing
enough to sustain the knowledge we all long to escape
I will be the life I've searched for
and I will tear this ground apart

New Lust

there are those rare moments
when the light is beginning to fall away
and the darkness illuminates every tiny detail
moments of solitude
that just wrap their spider like arms around me
the comfort that comes so sweetly in the word alone
the feeling of all the days prior
simply sinking into an empty bliss
this is what love feels like
I can feel the dark creep up around me
I can feel the embrace of everything
as it closes in
the threads of unhappy bliss
that slowly engulf me
and guide me home
and as the last of the light dwindles
and I find myself finally alone in the darkness
I can finally exhale
and let the depths take me in
a child that has finally found its way home

Typically

the sincerity your eyes once held,
the truth of lips and eyes
has vanished
leaving nothing but placation
and mistruths in its wake
you were once a sunrise in my eyes
a sweetness I didn't deserve
you have become the unlevel step in my life
the thing I forget about until I trip over it
I thought you were the diamond in the rough
but alas
you're a typical stepping stone
waking up to harsh realizations
is never a good way to start the day

Musically Relevant

I find my father resides in these notes
the ones I see played on your face
the twang of a single string
the way your tongue rolls over the words
the memory of what life was once

Melodious Stroke

you will drown in meaningless caress
a plea for help from the heavens
a melodious stroke
that you will only know
when the fingertips
finally unite
with that ungodly growl
from
deep
within

The smallest part

just a tiny piece
the smallest part
the least important thing
that's what I want
in all of this
something tiny
and
unimportant
that will mean the world to me
like invisible dinosaurs
and the wretched death of great literature

Factuation

there is genius in me somewhere
I feel it
I feel an ache of deprivation telling me
to dig in and rip it out
taking it all with me
I found the root of the problem
fed it, watered it
and let it grow into this
an in-factuation.
something that cannot be fully explored with only ten fingers.

Musical Alliance

a slow sigh,
the heave of shoulders,
this will be my one dedication,
to you,
you're my favorite part of everyday,
I'm looking for a tornado,
can you be mine?
Or is this where you lie?
I need fingertips slowly caressing thighs,
I need to be lifted,
into the depth of all we might be,
sucked in,
shattered,
and left astray,
the crescendo was worth it.

Momentary Stranger

There is beauty in your eyes
It sets the landscape ablaze
even when the scene is average

Your composition is perfect
There is a light to you
that I believe you don't see
Your tongue quivers in anticipation
when you're in the midst of a wonderful explanation
I can see longing in your eyes
when you talk of the women
that have graced and loved you
and your life
There is so much in store for you
and you, my friend
will find what you are looking for
in every regard
You should be the light of your life
don't ever let anyone make you believe you are less than amazing

Spider Mums

shall we string together words
in a pleasing fashion
allude to moments to come
Our best show of bedroom eyes
we could be magnificent within each other
My fingers could be like blooms on a spider mum
as they grow around you
engulfing you
the smell of growth in the air
soil and damp
You should be my spring time
every day of the year

Dr.Scholls

a sea full of curves
I'm caressed by underarms and misplaced calves
we rise in tandem
and fall so hard
faces masked
fingers grasping at a sense of truth
this will be the truth of us as a whole
we will find redemption in soft strings
that drive us into fluster
the gaps of our hands filled by strangers
that feel the same as empty spaces
some things can only be filled by solitude
but it will take us decades to know that
and in the meantime
we will try
we will be open hearted
and give up everything
to try to fit our feet
into that glass slipper
It turns out
there is no fit to the slipper
we all fit into it
if we want to
and I don't
I want to be the pumpkin
I want to be the thing that carries us to romance
up until midnight
we rise together

Evan

I cannot tell you
that you are the light of my life
that you have set the bar for every man
you are the what that drives me
to succeed
despite the endless barrage of ill fate
you are my muse
my one and only
try as I might
I can find no other
I cannot tell you any of this
because if you knew
I would be left defenseless
to you
and all that I pretend you don't mean to me

Hooks

I will eat your tongue
right out of your mouth
I will become your tongue
provide your nourishment
I will be your bridge to the world
I will sleep inside of you
I will live inside of you
I will see the world through your mouth
I will be your parasite
let's co-evolve baby

The Jerk of Breathing

and then
then there is that moment
the fish hook at the corner of your eye
that jerks the tears from that well
The one you try to never tap
but now
hearing this
I'm finally able to find depth
to this breath
I was lost in the shallows
until you coaxed me into the deep
and it's here
in the deep end
that I can just tread the sludge that surrounds me
I can stay above water here
It's tiring
and gruesome
but I know
that in order to drown I have a long way to go
I'm home in the depths

Spiritual Puppetry

this is what happens
when you allow yourself to be happy.
the world seems to slowly crumble beneath you
you can feel the plummet
the air engulf your body
and send your soul thrusting upward
at that moment when you let go
and exhale in submission
allowing yourself freedom
you are lifted by the catch of the air
in the feathers of wings
the slow glide upward as they slowly unfold
from the midst of your spine
it's the sensation of spiritual puppetry
the pull towards the heaven
the sail set to keep you moving towards....

Annihilation

as I removed the tentacles from about my neck
and took in the scent of a city burning
I could do nothing
but feel blessed
the intoxication of desire has got me hooked
I want to move about you
be the water on your fins
the caress that wakes you early in the morning
the person that loves you in the shadows
I will balance you
find your place within the totem
of me

The Finger of Discontent

the contortion of muscle
laid in the framework of what is supposed to be
a note gone wrong
here is where we find the sour taste of longing
that taste will continue to lay,
no,
lie underneath every succulent moment I have
you have
and will culminate in moments
of nothing
and nowhere
this is where we will live
in the garden of fingertips
and the lust for something that doesn't exist
we will be beautiful in those rare moments of glory
beauty will take on a new
conceptual novice
we will find ourselves lost
in the place we dislike so whole heartedly,
each other's eyes

Tactile

you didn't see me
I couldn't accommodate you
empowerment is the gift I bring
I've placed my hands upon yours
and forced the knots from within
taught you with meticulous detail
how to feel the canvas
your manipulation
was weak wristed and lacking of substance
a minor failure piled among loss
a tiny failure to be had

Truh love

If you alleviate my illness
allow me a breath of fresh air
I will feed and shelter you
I will allow you access to the flesh of my soul
I can be your host
your protector to the world
and you can gnaw me from the inside out
I'm waiting
for you to slide your hooks into me
you can be my cure

Stain

The memory swelled
I caught a tiny particle of the past on my tongue
and it exploded into longing
a nuclear assault upon my senses
You hold your woman like a pen
something to leave your mark with
a tool of expression
You grind her into the fibers
just enough to leave a mark
Nothing but a smudge on your scroll

If you were...

If you could only be right for me
lose here and gain there
I've been there
lived there
there is no room for if you were....
I will concede
give up and let go
I've been so willing
and you do nothing but let me know
let me know what's gone wrong
I wish for magnificence
the magnificence of just me
I don't want to change
I want nothing more
you're perfect
for me
I have to change
so
I will settle
because you're the best there is
I miss acceptance
the sacrifice is monumental
I could just be loved the way I am
or not at all
being alone
forever
isn't that bad
I can adjust

Heard Garden

I could hear you grow
I could taste the movement
I smelled the tumultuous earth
writhing with the seeds as they gave birth
I saw the roadways and stretch marks of growth
I saw the whole world culminate in a single prick of color
that announced a new life

Asthma

here is a sigh of relief
That never comes
I can't seem to find the air to exhale
Everything feels stagnant and overly ripe around me
The loss is palpable
I need something to inspire
something to inspire respiration
something that I can force my hands into
something that I can build
something I can taste the texture of
Cracks and crevices my tongue can be forced into
I need tentacles that can reach up
through me, into me
and really fondle my mind

Untitled

melodious sedation
the moments of fingertips
along the curves of a body
a breathing instrument
the sound of wood intruding on the taste of whiskey

Darkened Divinity

the beauty can literally be unbearable
where is the darkness?
the depth? the storm that arises from day after day of living?

tones of lackluster sacrifice
mixed with a baritone epitaph
the darkened divinity of someone with a cause

tactile encounters laced with subdued nuance
the faint scent of tea lingers on skin
the simple caress of a tongue
in the nape of a neck

Stuck in the Trap

I am lost
in your eyes
and mind
but was promised so many things
I was promised love
I was promised gratitude
the truth is
I never loved you

I wanted to be someone
someone I could not
I loved you when I needed to
I felt you when I had to
you followed in your father's footsteps
I loved shannon, heidi, and chelsea
you were my normality
Thank you for being that man

I Found It

once in a while
it all pours forth
I'm scared
I'm worried that all the things I covet
and love
are wrong and unhealthy
I don't know how to be me
I secretly long for...the missing piece
i thrive in chaos
and I'm in love
and it's all so complicated
how do people do this?
I should have this figured out by now
does it ever get better?
I miss Happy
I miss being married
I miss my siblings
the ones living and dead
I feel like there is no place for me
I still think about being gone everyday
Goddamnit
the things I don't understand are insurmountable
everything seems impossible
every day
I want someone to tell me
that this is all normal
that it all gets better
I just need someone to tell me...
it's not in vain

The Pride Lain at Your Feet

slain, disheveled and lacking in every aspect
hoping to understand what the touch of a hand can do for me
and finding nothing
exhausted in the hope of need

the wrinkles of your neck
that you hate
are what I love about you
watching you run your fingers up and down
hypnotizes me
and all I can think about is the lobe of your ear
and how sweet it feels on my tongue

The Feet of Mountains

I have Hope
I have Faith
I carry them
on each arm
they reside
in the creases of my elbows
they travel
to my shoulders
they occur in the warmness between my thighs
they flow through me like
blood
I feel hope in every moment
mostly the bad ones
I have hope
it will be okay
I have faith
I know it will be okay

Let's Play Pretend

be glad someone feigned loved
be happy no one keeps their eyes open for you
be ecstatic that no one will love you
then come home
realize
everyone lets you down
know it's not just you
me
all of us
being left alone is how we live
I ask for comfort
I get a moment
you don't try
and there is no need
it's not enough anymore
   one night
one fucking night

Confusion

a new set of limbs tossed about you
these are them
the moments you look back on
the pale glow of morning
as it spreads like roots taking to soil
the sun running through the cracks like rain
things creep slowly in the early hours on any day
the landscapes slowly shifting
fingers become vehicles to dreams
and as the momentum slows
you can feel the shift
right before you kick into gear
and coast slowly sown the other side

Greedy Little Phalanges

I've been torn in half
I can feel the greedy little digits gripping my flesh
I am left exposed
my heart literally a failing useless organ
left askew to be consumed by carrion
feeling my flesh slowly consumed
from my almost lifeless body
feeling myself eaten alive
is less painful than enduring your loss of love
and the turn to bitter hate

Two Weeks Notice

I will try
I will try to live
with this
this absence of love
I will find a place to dwell
I will fall apart
 But I will do it with strength
as much as I can muster
and will do it with honor
I will fall apart
I will lose everything
I will regret a minute and a half of lust
that I traded for a lifetime of black feathers
this will hang over me
it will bite my ankles at every step
There have been a lot of barriers
I have surpassed them all at some point
This, however, is insurmountable
I am not qualified
I'm giving notice

The Need

the sense of entire loneliness
is overwhelming
I need to be embraced
I need someone to hold me
I need someone to cup my belly
I need someone to understand I have never felt this before
but it's too much
I realize no one could love me that much
I have never felt less significant in the scheme of things
I almost pray for complications
leave me happy
let me know I could have
I just want someone special

Despite

ripped from grasp
left in a state of incongruous mayhem
I wander lost
I have no grasp of which way to turn
or how to get home
if I had one to get to
can I find comfort walking this path alone?
should I try?
or shall I just surrender now?
what's left at the end of the day?
not much anymore
even small comforts have left my path
there will be no comfort on this journey
every direction will be the wrong way
some are just destined for this path
prayers seen are only lost thoughts now
despite the utter loss of hope
I find myself grasping at the edges
just hanging on

Starving

the curves of your body call to me
I see emaciation fall before me
 I need this
you may be the last decent soul walking this road
I am in need of a decent soul
something to fuel my pace
something to nourish this black pit
something to call home while I slowly eat my way through it
may I take up residence within you?

Eyelids

joy resounds
I sometimes find it written so well within me
the celebration of tiny achievements runs through my joints
and trembles at my fingertips
the fulfillment,
the excitement of the genuine
veins pumping the nutrition of sustenance
The revival of an artist lost that has been found
I had become so.. innate
sometimes it takes very little
just the tiny curve of an eyelid
to renew the sense of self
I have found my art
once again
at least for a moment
I am me

Sandcastles

my body swayed
I felt the depth of myself
I have never been one that believes in true love
but I felt
so much
I felt this life wrap around me
comfort me
and fill me so deep that it spilled out

in the end
there was nothing left
but you and I
the tide washed upon the shore
and erased everything
I miss being part of a sand castle wonderland
Even the imprint of our souls has gone

Straight down the middle

melodious fingertips
walking the tracks of every composition
my fingers feel like rusty train cars
I no longer care for the track
I no longer feel the journey
just the ridges that come with details
the rust is the detail
 I can't forget
beauty among destruction
horrible beauty

Made

this life is done well (unwell)
I'm blessed by guilt
I should have done better
I tried
I swear
today was renown by a thousand sunsets and a million waves
and all of them seemed insignificant
I took ten steps on to the beach
and realized I was alone
I was happy then
because there was no more lack of everything
there are moments unprecedented
and I wasn't sure where to go
There were small things I knew I wanted to be
and big things I know I didn't
and it all brought me home
and during that 30 seconds
if I had ever seen waves
they were crashed upon my feet
I literally felt hopelessness made
and it made me feel very uncomfortable
I hope that right now
I can do everything past that

Above It

being struck by the extraordinary is easy
being struck by the ordinary
takes a keener eye
It's the little things that count I suppose
Can you imagine how much it takes just to proceed with life
every day, for some
Life is shit
Its rarely kind
and no one ever said it would be easy
the rewards are rarely exceeded by the downfalls
and yet
I see people every day
that are just thankful
that their heads are still above the quicksand

Monet too close

and there we went
lost in oblivion
conversations over loaded with over justification
but all that mattered
is we were there
along with dali, pollack, and fucking monet
I would love to be an artist
but I find my role models lacking
I would love to be the person that fell asleep painting
made excuses
and never accomplished anything
except
a small amount of insight
it's hard to knock another artist
when you love them
envy them
I'm the next Picasso (so depressing)

Hinges gone wrong

there is something
I feel behind my eyes
when my soul feels heavy
and my words feel weak
The feeling that wells up
like a backed up drain
not overwhelmed...
but aware of the dire circumstances of life in general
I know it's time to hike up my socks
zip up my boots
and tackle this thing called living
there will be so many obstacles
so many battles lost
so many days where just coming home is painful
but
there will also be
lovely dismay
beauty among death
and painful normalcy.
I find myself ecstatic just to be part of it
So, on days like this
where all the news was bad
and it was far too windy to be publicly irritated
I will find joy in some really good orange chicken
and the humor of a world blown off its hinges

Fall

fall into me
melt over every part of my body
be the thing that covers my skin
my limbs. my digits
just for tonight

Dungeons

feeling intrusive
on moments you never belonged in
I wasn't ready to be back here
and I think I might never be
the bed that used to reel me in
no longer seems
intimate
I find myself attempting to reassert myself in this home
I'm a lost page
a lost book mark
my place has been sacrificed and forgotten
and its only 24 hour detention
the dice has been rolled
my night is over
everything I craved for this evening
is lost
sacrificed to childhood games
tomorrow I will finally grow up
break ties
and leave this all behind

Water Color on Vellum

I'm a cephalopod trapped in a bi pedal land dwelling mammals body

Water Color

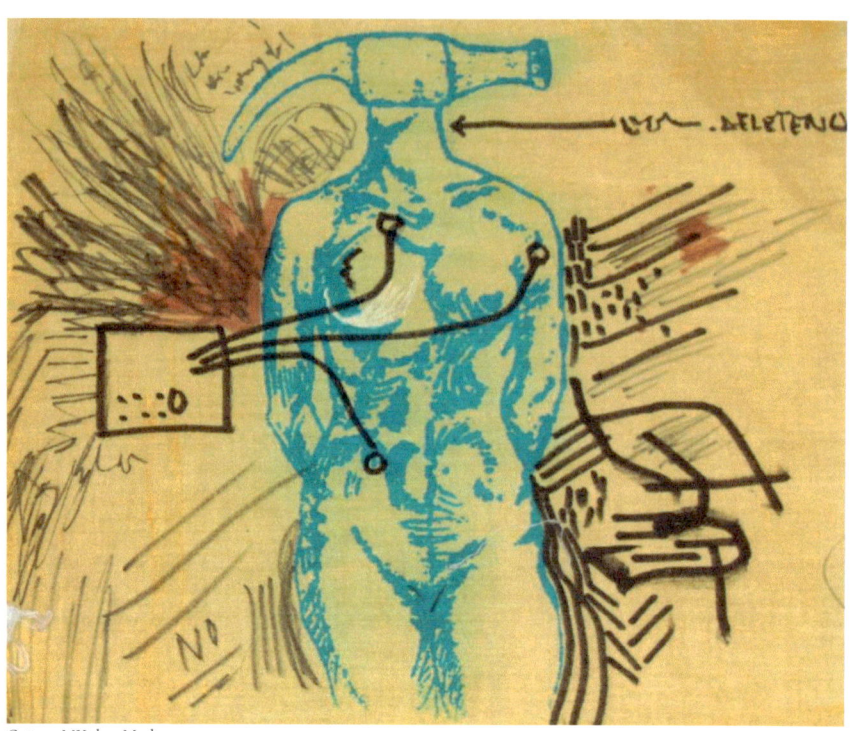

Cotton, MX dye, Marker

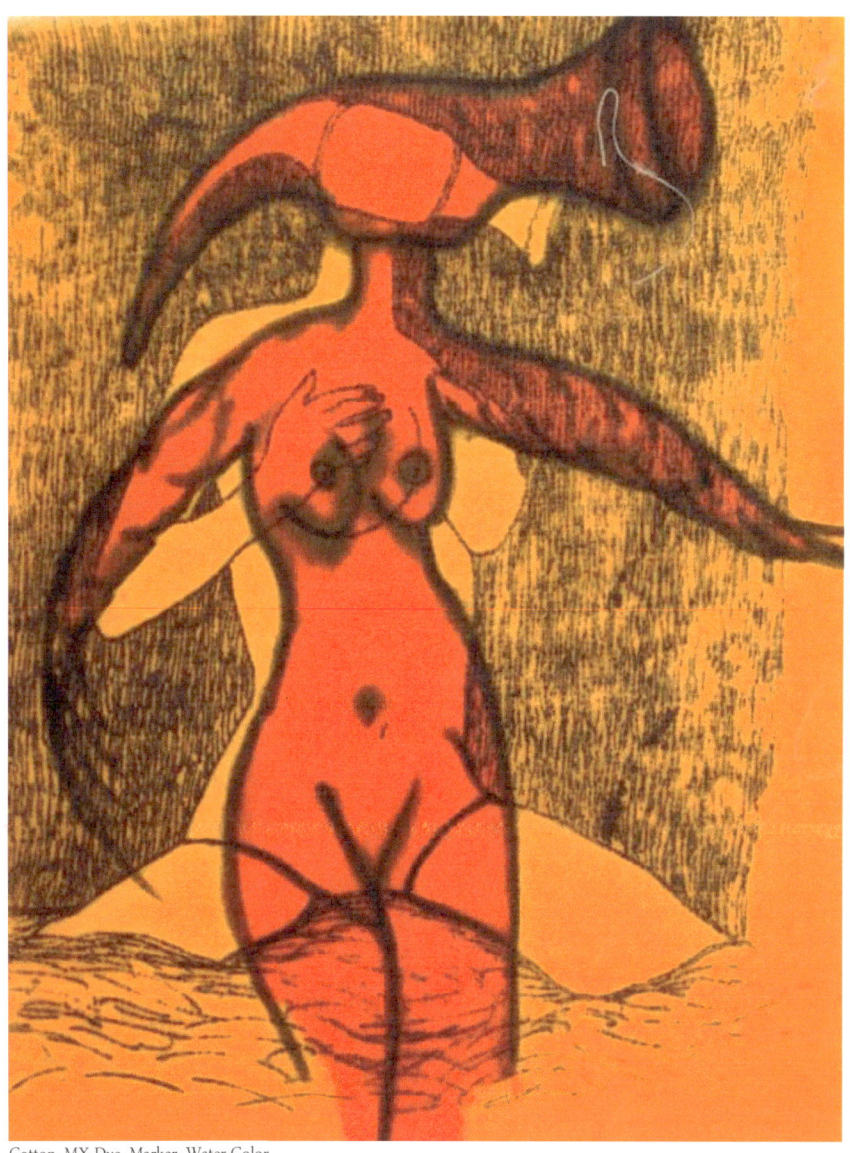

Cotton, MX Dye, Marker, Water Color

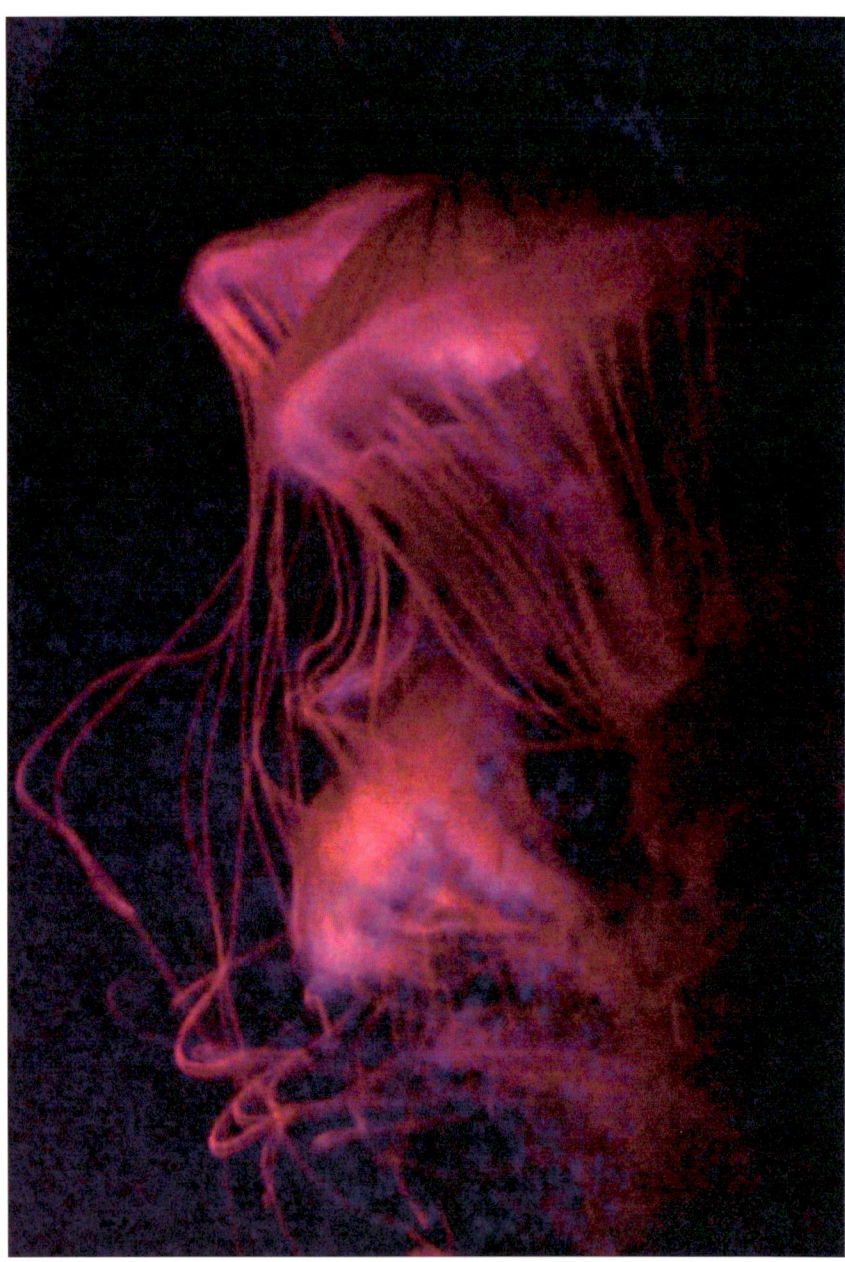

Photograph

I'm a cephalopod trapped in a bi pedal land dwelling mammals body

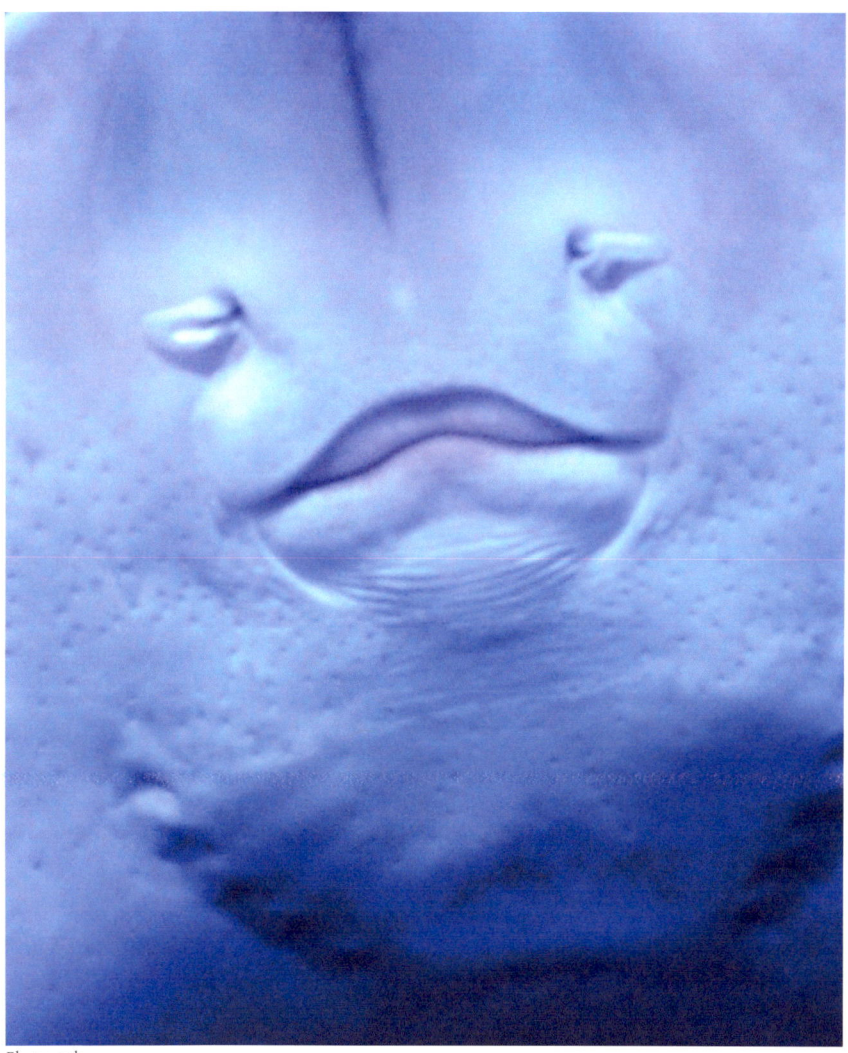

Photograph

Mixed Media

I'm a cephalopod trapped in a bi pedal land dwelling mammals body

Water Color

Water Color

I'm a cephalopod trapped in a bi pedal land dwelling mammals body

Water Color

Water Color

I'm a cephalopod trapped in a bi pedal land dwelling mammals body

Photograph

Water Color

India Ink

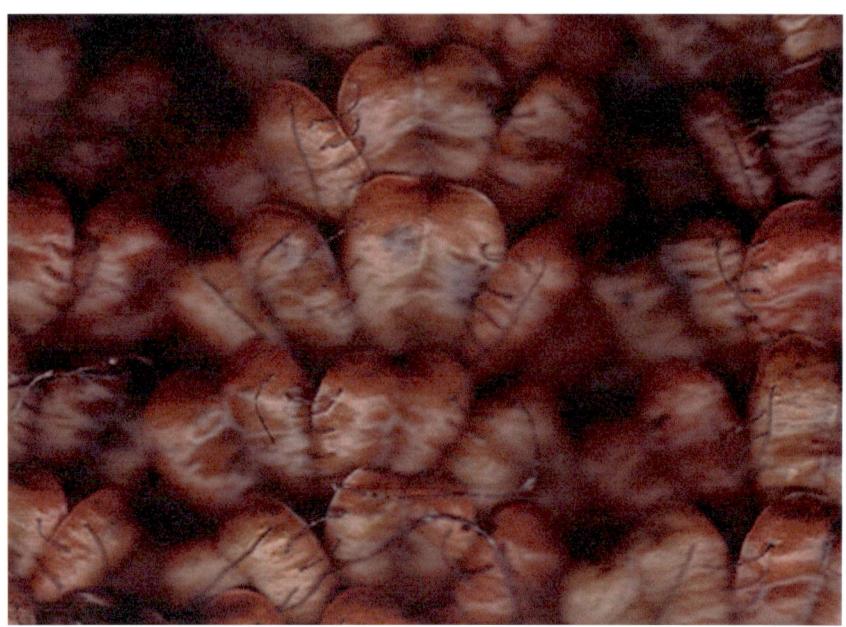

Pods, cotton thread, wax

I'm a cephalopod trapped in a bi pedal land dwelling mammals body

Photograph

Water Color, pastel, acrylic

I'm a cephalopod trapped in a bi pedal land dwelling mammals body

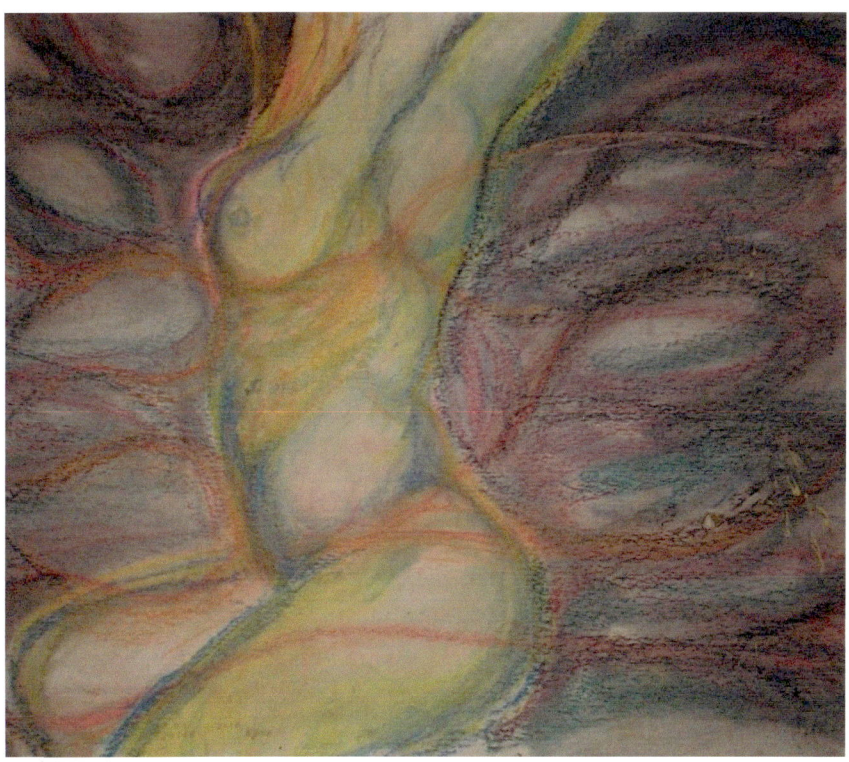

Pastel

Photograph

I'm a cephalopod trapped in a bi pedal land dwelling mammals body

Colored Pencil

Photograph

I'm a cephalopod trapped in a bi pedal land dwelling mammals body

Photograph

Photograph

I'm a cephalopod trapped in a bi pedal land dwelling mammals body

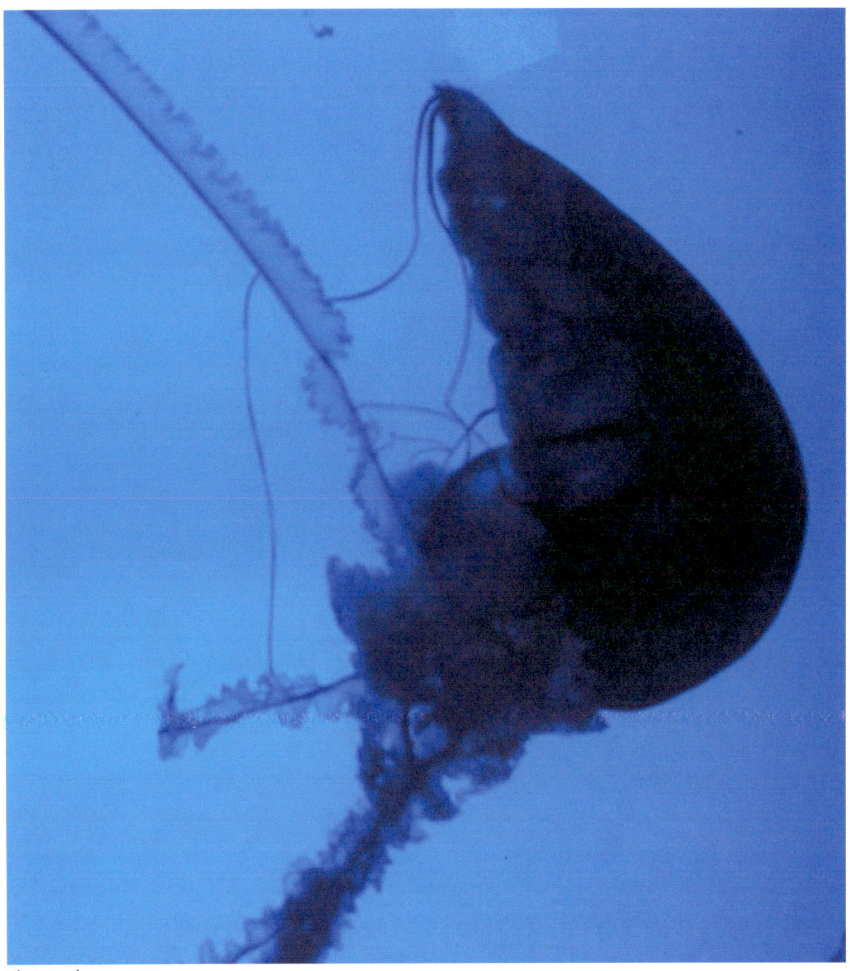

Photograph

Photograph

I'm a cephalopod trapped in a bi pedal land dwelling mammals body

Photograph

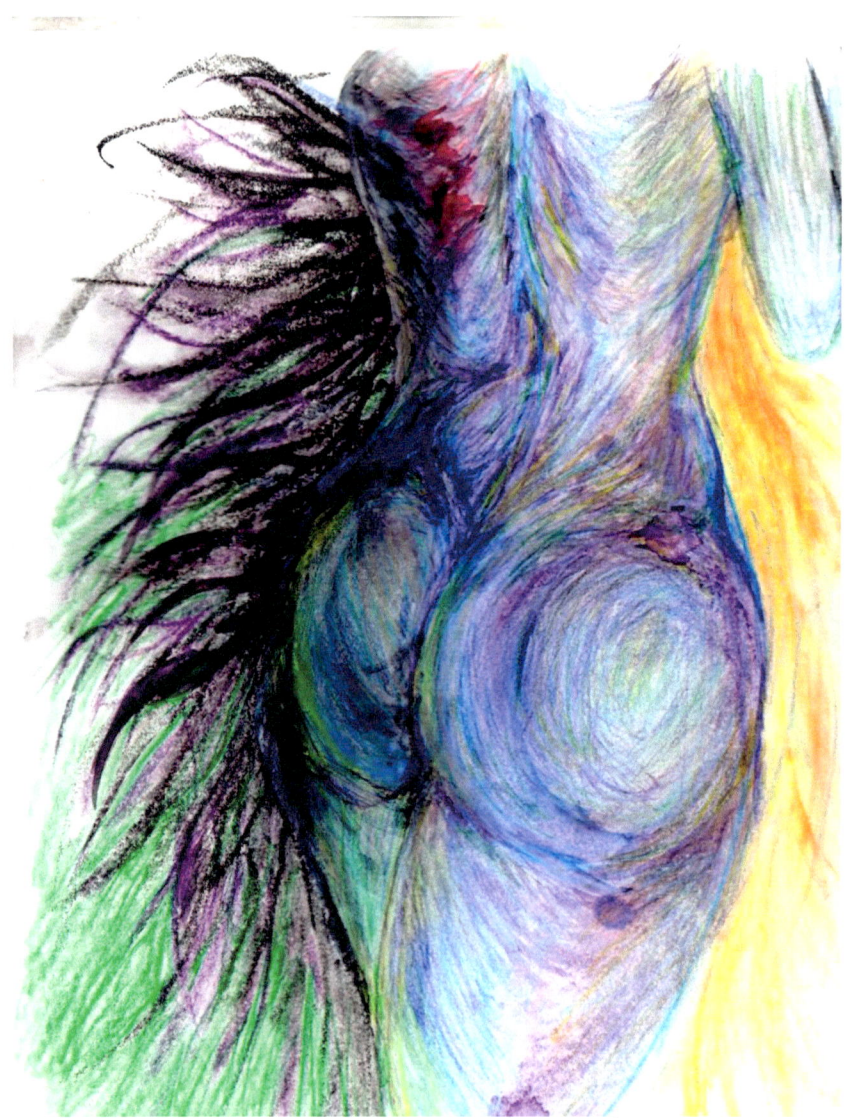

Pastel, colored pencil, water color, marker

Drawing by Kelly Pennington

Mundane Company

drafted and planned interactions
that seem to go wayward
unknown friends and unplanned circumstances
finding peace in moments lost to intervention
here we are and here we be
and the moments that soon follow will make or break
an evening
happy birthdays
and all the unhappy days that followed
let's make a toast to future mistakes
and hopefully the lack thereof
we can all find friendship
and relief at the end of a bottle
or several of them
all the best eras begin at the ending of another truly great one
and an era has ended
youth is gone
only adults remain
and what will we all do with ourselves now?
become teachers? lawyers? parents? lost souls looking for
space in an overcrowded world.
we will do what every person before us did
try our best to be happy
fight for excitement in a mundane world
my fight, my battle, has led me here
and you are the one that has waited for me
brought the significance of daily life
so here is to you
and survival in the midst of every mundane moment
you have set all those moments ablaze

I Wasn't There

i feel like the illegitimate child of loss and despair
i have no business being here
this moment has done nothing for me
except ease the problems that come with attachment
i dont bring love home
because there is no home for love in my midst
i prefer love from afar
very far
love, simply put, is just a bad idea
its said
its done
lets all go home
avoid eye contact
and pretend this never happened

Battle Plan

the fuse has been submerged
there will be no explosion
its been quelled
its over
i officially wave the white flag
in enemy territory
i have lost the battle, today
but there will be another soon
and we learn from every attack
i know where to set up barriers now
and where i can mend the wounded
Its been some time
but im sure i can withstand one more battle
maybe two
if im lucky
while i surrender today
the troops are preparing for tomorrow
you win some, you lose some
tomorrow
i will win, despite the odds

Drowning in yesterday

I'm floating
it's all gone weightless
yet I feel myself sinking
the water above is ablaze
with every coal and ember
I have left
I'm going under this evening
I will drown
i will lose the part of me where you reside
or used to
In the morning
I will wake up
and daily life will resume
but tonight
I will think of you
i will think of your arms around me
the safety I felt in your presence
i will be reminded that you made me smile
when i least wanted to
and I will send all my prayers and good graces to you
you will be there, in my top ten moments
in the list of people i adored
I hope when this all ends
i will see you tower over me once again
I'm sorry i couldn't do more
just remember
you were loved
here
for a moment

Kristopher

Have you ever been disappointed?
i don't mean by the menial things
the small disappointments we all suffer everyday
but truly let down
forty five minutes before i was let down
we were sitting in the car
talking about butterflies
the kind you get in your stomach
the first time you meet someone you can see a future with
fifteen minutes before i was let down
we were laughing
i was trying to be serious
and i complained about people never trying hard enough
and five minutes before i was let down, I was alone
waiting
and you just never returned.
Now it's been hours since I was let down
and I'm home, without you
I have to decide what to do with your things
and who to call
I feel A little empty knowing you're never coming back here
I should have listened to my parents

Lost in the Cushions

too late to tell
where things have gone
or where they might go
wanderlust for all the moments forgotten and long gone
left wanting
lost in what might become of us all
there are many things missing
but soul
my soul isn't one
i can smell the love in my home'
now
and every day that follows

the imagination open
at last
welcome to the front
sleeping alone in crowded rooms
it gets tiring
i have no idea what to feel anymore
i haven't moved in days
yet i find myself lost on the path
i just keep wandering
wondering
and so the journey continues
pray for the best

Comfort in Vein

we all find guilt in the eyes of our peers
it is only those closest
our loved ones
our family, our lovers
that truly find the innocence in our eyes
in our expressions, in the quiver of a note lept forth
its in that sincerity, that love
that i say my blessings every night
i know, that no matter how large the trespass
or the charges lain at my feet
there are people
that hold me in hope
that love me in vain
and that is where i find my comfort
unconditional love, can be so conditional
but, there is a place
we all live there at times
Its the comfort of knowing you can meet the conditions
of the people you love
because you love them so truly
its the reflection of you in another person's eye
the twinkle of your reflection
thats the truest of all comforts
and I,
love
dwelling there

Lost Again

its cavernous
this life and its foot holds
its easy to get stuck in the wrong place
with no way up or down
all of us have taken the wrong path at one time
its the amount of time you spend on that path that separates us
some of us turn around and ask for directions right away
others just enjoy the scenery
some of us just dont care
we never turn back
after all the wrong path is still a path
just remember,
at the beginning of the path is a crossroads
and what direction you choose
is not nearly as important as the people
that you meet at the beginning of the path
they will be what define the journey
and thats the most important part of a hard road
the people that make it seem worthwhile

The Songstress

She waved her big leaden hips
swain like a flag
gripping the music
and drawing it in
to a part of her so deep
that it was like the breath in her lungs
brought in to feed life to every vain and molecule
exhalations of mingled notes and phrase
an offering to the heavens
to the gods

Curbside

i lay my hands down
right up on that bend in your neck
I feel a flush in my cheeks
the smoothness of your skin
its remarkable
I melt at the sound of your voice
to barely touch your chest
you seem to fit me
remarkable the way pieces can fit in the wrong puzzle

Empty Vessel

Coherency is wonderful in small doses
i see where im going and dont like it
i have no one to cling to for help
i wish you were the one
but i know youre not
never will be
i need some greatness
its never coming
i cant be a vessel anymore

Unseen

Saw it
in a way i have never seen it before
i was wrong
there is hope
its in you
Its everywhere I should have looked
I should have known you were the cure to the zombie apocalypse
my bad
sorry

Dependent

there is nothing new
sloth permeates every part of me
Ive rendered myself useless
passion seems unbearable
youth is exhausting
and the desire to grow up was lost on the battle field
Im officially lost in between
there are so many things I thought permanent
that just fade and wane in time
Have you ever wished for something rancid just to get through the day?
something monumental?
I propose this
everyone of use do something amazing
now
something worth talking about
If we all do something small
we may build a monument together
you are all the mortar between my bricks
Youre what i depend on to stand strong
dont let me down

The Traveler

To be cured of lust is like a horrible lobotomy
there is this sense of something lacking
but its hard to put your finger on
A missing puzzle piece on a project almost complete
Ive lost lust..
not just for you, or her
but for it all
I miss the curves of an instrument in my arms
and the sounds of a women well caressed
That feeling
right before you embark on a wonderful piece of music...
the feeling afterwards of rubbing my shoulder where a neck once
rested
I know where this road leads
and i know there will always be bumps and ditches
but i think i need to leave the city and get back to the unpaved
I might find my lust there
waiting
side of the road
thumb in the air

Roots

I need to return to my roots.
I need to plant myself in the soil beneath you and
sprout up through toes and wrap around feet and ankles.
I need to pull your hips towards the sun and
tie my vines around your thighs.
I need to drink the nutrients from your body
and lightly caress your breasts with my leaves.
I need to grow with you, from you, in you.
I will wrap myself around you
I will grow on you
I will drain you
and eventually sacrifice you...
to
my own personal growth.

Mealtime

Its unfortunate
but this is it
youre my people
this is my place
The strangest part is that I love it here
I would not trade this for anything
I find myself smiling more than ever before
i feel rebuilt
remade
and I have you
all of you to thank
you made me who I am now
and i cant imagine anything more magnificent

Amy

To touch a young persons skin
the taughtness of the flesh
to smell the youth of them pouring from every pore
Its like touching something valuable that you know does not
belong to you
there a certain desire to run away with it
have you ever experienced something so intoxicating it was hard
to walk away?
But you...you are different.
I can see your youth.
I hear it in the words coming from your mouth.
Your eyes say something very different.
The underneath when the layers are pulled away speaks an
ancient language.
you should let the layers drop.
peel away the mask.
youre much more beautiful underneath the youth.

I can see the depth of you.
dont let me be the only one

Dark ages

sex once poured from my fingertips
there were luscious over ripened phrases
that leapt around me in every direction
the call of the may pole
now im surrounded by nothing but sense
the constant bombardment of an everyday life
the intimacy has changed to the familiar
my connections have stopped being the pure physical
and slowly graduated to those of support and...
love.

its as if I was living in the dark ages and have suddenly passed
into an age
of trust and innocence.
people are kind and connected to me in ways
i cannot sever
The problem is...
i preferred the torture, unknowing and death of the dark ages.
But alas, how does one return to that time?
Once you have the knowledge of what things can be
its dangerous to tread into the waters of what things were.

Join me

there is a temptation i cannot describe
i cannot find the words
i dont know where it comes from
it feels like being eaten from the inside out
i feel bitten
and struck with a great fever
from the wound all that pours forth is rejected emotion
and a dislike of humanity in general
and yet
i am humanity and this is where i thrive

so right here
right now
i shall begin this journey
Care to join me?

Burn Victim

I will be left to my own devices night after night
in the solitude of mishap
I will play, pull and break all strings that keep me connected
I have learned to love solitude
solitude, loneliness and the strength to embrace both
is what makes me capable
it is the state that allows me to handle disaster
It is how i manage to be found when all is lost

Lost children

I will never know the answer
i will never know the reasons
I may never know why I am who I am
but i will know gratitude
I will know love
i will know how to live and love
and in happiness in this confusion
I will understand the touch of sweetness
and the burn of remorse

No Names

to miss someone
to miss you down to the depths of my soul
the depths of this life
i know that life goes on
but
there are moments when i know
you should be here
and there is no one to share...
all of this with
im all alone without you
to simply have a thumb brushed across my brow
and hear
"i know, I know youre here"
just to be seen
I fear that without you
I may never be seen again
i need someone to see the loveliness through all this sadness
and im afraid
that will never happen
I am....without you

Exclamations

Dealing with individuals that function within opposites
knowing grace has fled and wondering when hope will once again
be clear
How does one divulge a lifetime of secrets to people that only
feign interest?
The love of convenience is rarely that way in the end
and as I gaze upon a scrap of lost
lost interest
i wonder, will i ever be worthwhile?
Most likely not
yes we wane and people age, yet intentions never change
and i often find myself lost wading knee high among them
prayers go unanswered and yet we continue to offer them to the
heavens
or the nothingness, just the void, depending on a point of view.
I lose myself everyday
within myself and this burden of disdain
to just dabble is to fail
or so I hear
i shall fall to waste amongst friends and lovers
I shall lay down and be walked upon until I become stepping
stones
and one day
you will all grind me to dust beneath your heels
realizations that the method direct is never the best one chosen
discomforting truths and then the understanding
of simply less than
Oh the things that fall within and upon a mind felt with unease
What is the moment, the second, that made you check
either [] yes or [] no?
why is there never a maybe?
shall we all be undone by the doings of others?
or will there be that moment,
that fantastic fucking moment where we all exclaim,
"fuck it"
and just let go?

Self-serving

The sound of an image
the shattering of a concept
misdirected affections and the disdain of familiarity
the worst part of every relationship
is discovering
who the other person really is
the complexity and ability
of individuals to manipulate
each other to serve themselves
is astounding

All Hallows Eve Again

every year
i sit in remorse
and remember unfortunate moments and unloving words
i miss you greatly
i am so sorry for my unkindness that evening
i didnt know
i was too young to understand
i look for your face every hallows eve
i have yet to spot you
but i know you are out there
you have always been
and always will be the sweetest sight i have ever seen
i will miss you tonight
as i have every night for years now
you were lovely
and every redeeming part of me came from you
should you ever choose to haunt a house
look me up
I'll be here

Dogtopia Of Highlands Ranch

bring it here
let me look
is that comfort in your hand
may i hold it?
on the day you go
take me with
in spirit
in nature
to have the mind that breathes
and swallows creativity is a blessing
to have that mind and work at dogtopia
is a death sentence
dont think
pay no mind to the camera
make it look good
seeing people care so much
and get paid so little
by the way...this email constitutes your third write up
youre basically a glorified fast food agent
i have no use for you

Ties

a hand
a neck and
an ear
everywhere i want to be
and everything to keep me from it
running sacrifices
slit stitches
loveless mournings

I Want...

to be saved....
once.
Come to my aide
i have never and will never ask this again
but tonight
save me
from myself, here, now
I will send one tiny SOS
thats all i can give
come my way
i need you
right now
message unreceived
i will be alone through every moment

Red Rover

Red rover Red rover
send that son of a bitch life right over
he always runs too hard
and hits the weakest link
always seems to break through

The exhaustion of being touched all day
it gets to you
It changes who i am and how i feel
I am a lifeless lump of clay being molded everyday by every
interaction

Insult to injury

I love that feeling
standing on the ledge
arms out
looking down the world seems so menial
do you ever hear a song in the breeze?
its so melodic and every note is far too crisp
looking up i see only promise and beauty
The answer to getting up is traveling down

you are told all growing up
that you can be anything if you put your mind to it
its so far from the truth its almost insulting

The Kiosk

i wish for eight arms
tentacles enough to grasp all those i love
a leash rendered from desire
in arm's length as the expression goes
sailors believed octopi were good luck
i simply believe we would all be better with 8 arms
its the ability to grasp many things at once
which is literally the concept of intelligence
i can barely wield two arms and a mouth
i want understanding
i want to know where im going
and im almost certain, I cannot get that information here

Second Place Ribbons

ahhhh
the sounds of settling into discomfort
there is nothing more tantalizing than the comfort of loneliness
to just wallow for an evening in my own short comings
the soundtrack that drives me to celebration when coming in
second place
i may never reach great heights
but i will live every day like the last in the deepest depths
its only here, in the heartbreak of my life
that i can touch that eternal flame
the one burning faintly below me
and it is that
that tiny flicker at the end of the deepest tunnel
that keeps me coming back for more

In Tact

i watch us all unfold
among each other
i watch the graceful ballet of interactions
i see the mishaps and mistakes
i appreciate those moments
they make me feel human
they make me feel flawed
lately i see nothing but imperfections
and they seem to make me feel at home
the broken banister thats led up the stairs my entire life
the lack of something sturdy to grasp
like walking an old bridge made of planks and withered ropes
my heart skips a beat with just the idea of losing my foothold
will i make it to the other side in tact?
only the journey knows the ending

My Monster love

tiny rivulets, sinew, rivers of marrow and stitches
handiwork lain in love
of love
mending of scars melded with creation itself
the electricity of life
the moment where the creature comes alive in your gaze
in your eyes
in mine
the terror torn with ragged loveliness
and the knowledge that all before and after embodies...
pure wretchedness
i will be yours,
your father, mother, lover
all that you could need
i will be all only to leave you in mourning
i will bring you here in splendid fruition only to abandon
you to
wretched realizations and harmful truths
you will be all that is great in me
and all that poisons my every breath
i will be your creator
and the death of us
baby, i will be your dr. frankenstein if you'll be my monster

Granulated

sandpaper kisses
paper cut love
the granulation of skin upon skin
waking up raw
love that grates upon us
finding ourselves ground down
 tiny pieces
ready for consumption
i will refine us
and this moment
finds me bore down to a minimum
im just powder
sugar upon your lip
simply wiped away by a flick of the tongue

All I want is You

i will lay down arms
and back away
i will wave that pale flag and cast my gaze below
i will do these things if it means you feel whole
and victorious once again
i long for your strength
find who you are so that i might find myself within you
you were once a foe i dare not reckon with
now you seem to me nothing but a minor inconvenience
where ever you have lost yourself
whatever the wound
please let me nurse this weakness from within you
so that i may once again face my only foe
and bring you back to this battle everlasting
i need a bloody and brutal test of strength
and the only force i long to tear apart
is you

Soap Operas and Fairy Tales

theres nothing better left
im reduced to text and eventual meetings
and son of god damned bitch
this is all there is for me
i will be with a man i dont love
dont want
forever
i dont know what the hell else to do
there was one
one man i felt compelled to be, just be with
and
he didnt want me
informs me daily he never will
theres nothing i can do
he doesnt want a life
a person like me
had she been 18
im sure she would be your everything equal
it hurts to feel lacking
because of someone that will never be as good as you are
but
like they say
these are the sand through the hourglass
the days of our lives

For my One and Only

i have curled my emotions around you
between us
i have felt your touch and your voice renew me
i can see words in your eyes
novels and fiction your smile
stories reign between your thighs
you were my press, my story not yet told
when the words were finally lain in ink
it was not what i believed it would be
it was engorged yet emaciated
it was a pearl made from filth
a pearl upon my tongue
a discomfort i didnt warrant
it was you my dear
it was the taste of scorn and disappointment

Jessup

shall we all just dismiss the past?
Live in today and dismiss memory?
forgiveness is given in an instant
should we not learn from these instances?
we allow ourselves to be taken
again and again
defeated with no winner
lets begin to cherish our allies in the way they deserve
no longer long for defeat behind their backs
let us begin to fold the masses within us
and find them kin
lets choose to truly love one another
even on the most menial basis
i will try
give it a shot
we might enjoy it

The general public

the mind is endless
and we go on despite no recognition
there is rejection and loss
and all that we can do is conquer it
or fold beneath it
i chose to conquer
i chose to remain a pillar
i will not fold, i will not crumble
i will remain
endless, obtained, unscathed
and never taken
by anyone less than me
i refuse to fold
i will keep my faith
despite trembling in my hands
and the pain in my side
i will be worthy despite my own questions
and allowances of defeat
I will be loved
and if not by you
then by someone greater
you have lost your hold on me

Some People's Children

god dammit
faith is nothing to be reckoned with
watching a loved one die pierces you to the deepest innards
she is my anchor
my calm in the storm
and the nastiest woman i have ever known
she is my mother
she inspires my hatred
and ignites my moments of love
I am lost as she

Im Leaving Now

i cannot leave you
there is no future
im living in a lost future
there is no place for me here
even when im broken i must coddle you
you have always been taken care of
I never have been
its my fault
but knowing that i mean less than meaningless worlds,
or drywall
makes me wonder if i was ever worth anything
i would guess not
i know
I love you because youre amazing
im just
worthless
so i understand why you treat me so
I allowed myself to see your innards
your mind, intelligence, gorgeous smile
you made me feel like
there was no real chance
i had so much faith
hope abounding
all rejected
i cant be here much longer
being uncared for is no longer my specialty
my heart is homeless
and yours carries nothing legitimate
i would step into that any day
 i was only amusing when i was new
i expected a pillar
a column
not someone to care for on a day filled with pain,
when does someone ask me if they can get me anything?

A good man

slipping into this past
the one i dont want
i find every moment incongruent
and awkward

i want you to be my equal
i want you to share it all
the dips and pulls
mood swings that come with us
and yet
i know its only you
my job is to accommodate and validate
yours is to let us know
that there is no way to live up
I love you from a part of me that i dont want to exist
for some reason i find myself within you
and you will never sacrifice a single thing for me
and thats what i have always had
so i have no reason to look for something different now
i had a gleam
i had a hope
you seemed like someone else
lost
one that doesnt exist
i felt intertwined with you
there is no us
just you
even the way your hands move
its uncaring
and now i know that
hope is scarred for a reason
and why faith is illegible
because they dont exist
they say good guys finish last
there are no good guys
the way you penetrate me is harsh
unclean
regardless
the emotional condition gone

The Note

take me
take a part of me
that will never return
take it far
and deliver it to people that need it
let me go
I have had mine
and i find myself done
i want to engulf you and this
this moment
i want to cover you in understanding
and let you know
that i understand your decision
i wont be here
when you return
they say all dogs go to heaven
im assuming that includes bitches

Paige Rodrigurez

youre young and believe you have all the answers
believe you know the world
but you have yet to plunge in to any part of it
youre lacking in every introspective tunnel
even the labels of your life attempt to carry weight they cannot
the next time you attempt to dominate me
or direct me in any manner
will be the last time
i can assure you that your youth and sweet lemon coated remarks
will not be heeded in my court
my little lady
you and your bastard are in for the run of your life

Dogtopium Madness

to stand amidst
a symphony made from a hundred voices
calling out all at once
all different languages
never understanding a word
a melody of noise
this is where i find myself
and i find it appealing in every way
i find myself reminded that
every soul
no matter how tiny
has the ability to lift another up
my body leaves this orchestra pit of chaos
and misunderstanding
everyday
feeling, tired and flimsy
and as my body screams in exhaustion
i find my soul lifted in joy
i have found my place
to every scratch and bruise
i give thanks

Just This

my eyelids droop
im falling into the abyss
of your shoulder
its the one place
the one moment
that i can be completely here
just me
i never thought i would find love
in a place that literally smells like an armpit
go figure
love is grand

Great Adventures

as a child
i used to dream of moments
beyond this universe
beyond me
i was taken away by every dream
as an adult
i see that
all those moments i dreamed
are less interesting
than those in front of me
i may never go far
i may never do much
but i will see you
i will see the complications of humanity
i will see the wonder of grief
i will see the love that dies and grows in death
i will see the thorns of the gardens of marriage
and i will know the beauty that occurs
in every childs eye
i will be blessed
here and now
and that, my friend, is the greatest adventure

Kobayashi Maru

the darkness upon new awakening
those moments with friends
lost
still present and not yet discovered
we shall all experience
these moments in solitude
it takes one second of shared interest
to placate a lifetime
of friendship
i continue to enjoy the moments
of open conversation
lost comments
to watch a man truly covet his woman
is still a lovely sight to see
and its enriching to have moments
lost within moments
kobayashi maru
it can only happen so many times
lets enjoy the one time we can all find success

Starting now

i left you
to finish my pain in solitude
i wanted to grant you peace
you had a long hard day
you feigned drowsiness

why not just venture home
my fuel is running low
and so is my tolerance

seeing you
wide awake
the light at the end of the bed
no recognition
of me in this home'
this house

i tell you
that youre an amazing man
but
i would like to see it
do you think its true?
  lets find out

can one man

ever be as sweet as i would hope
my past tells me no
my future'
tells me
no
you have one chance
it starts today

Sink In

walking among moments
lying among keys
among strangers
dangers you haven't known before
seeing where they take you
it will not be the moment you hoped for
and as you sink in
to their words
you hope to find yourself
but you just find that deep
felt sorrow
that's left with every encounter
so
sink in now
find that moment
within where you're at
and live it
to the end of your days
and hope that it makes you happy
and bring it home every chance you have
'cus that's what it means
to be us

Mud

oh
and we say this night is over
but i've found it just began
i'm finding so much love
in these moments hunting
and i'm finding moments
in your incongruity
and here we go again
sink in
bring it out
toes encased in mud
the feeling you get
of freedom granted
from one moment
of lost memories
and that you might find
hiding
in sandals and pajama pants
and tonight that's where i find myself
lost
in moments of joy and sorrow
and hoping
that tomorrow when i wake
these moments will still be here
right now
as i remember
finding the tide and flow
and realizing
where you lay
within that
and hoping
when we wake up in the morning
we still have these feelings
inside of us

To the Depths

Have you ever seen it?
I mean really seen it?
the way horror looks reflected in someone's eyes?
I have.
I have seen tragedy and despair
I have seen love and understanding.
i have seen all of these looks.
But terror
Terror is the look of someone that is aware
aware of whats about to come
and aware they wont survive it
That look
that look will break your heart
and destroy you to the depths

Heavy Metal

I was bound
I was chained to you like a dog in the dirt
Nothing to take me away except my view of the road
and the melancholy grip of your notes
I can feel the weight of the chain
even after its gone
That deep pull to the axis
the gravity just drags my hips towards the ground
everybody has their demons to fight
mine can pick a six string like ripe berries
notes so deep your eyes roll and your tongue thrusts forward
the heavy metal chain
just embracing me from head to toe

Dirt

and the sweetness abounds
fresh from that soil I had to turn up with my bare hands
I spend my days watching it
turn and shift
the worms sifting through those roots right beneath
each time I find my bare hands thrust into the earth
i find they take root
when i pull them free
i can only smell roots and redemption
the clay beneath my nails
reminds me

Spiderhood Dreams

You crept down
like a single teardrop
just suspended
your arms blindly feeling for a resting place
you fell so slowly
one foot touching the ground in trepidation
i saw you feel foundation
and let your limbs drop blindly
the tiny thud of your weight upon the world
I watched in amazement as you crept so slowly towards me
touching every cell as you stepped into my space
Youre an amazing intrusion
one i have been waiting for
Im so happy to see you here
just creep up
and crawl in
Ive been waiting for this invasion
for far too long

Tunnel Vision

and your notes came
so unexpectedly
Like a pause in the middle of the chorus

The light at the end of the tunnel
became so much less necessary
because the tunnel has become so familiar
I just turn my head lights on
and i follow the brake lights in front of me
and if this tunnel never ends
I could be happy here

That tiny light, right above the service door
the tunnel within the tunnel
where the maintenance men reside
that is my new bon fire
I will gather around it
with the strangers that stopped midway
and we will rise
and we will shine

There is a light now,
right in the middle of the tunnel
Its dim and miscolored
but its a place
to stop and rearrange
to look at the map
and recalculate the directions
Sometimes your destination changes midway
and sometimes,
the middle of the tunnel is the destination

Im waiting for you there
in the middle
I need someone to guide me towards the light

towards the exit

but,
we could just turn around
when we get there
and make the light at the end be the beginning of the end

The next end

Erosion

I was hoping for more than this
Something amazing
something worth while
but in this shallow water
everything seems murky
the sand kicks up in every direction
my movement in this space obstructs my view
all i can see is my footsteps being swallowed
I came here for clarity and new perspective
but my imprint is falling off the planet
and maybe
thats the gift
the tide is washing me away
If I stand here long enough
the sand will take every part
I will be washed away and worn to nothing
My bones could become the porous pebbles you walk on
I could be part of your shore
when you walk into the tide
a thousand years from now

The feel of my rock

I will grasp you in those moments where nothing is solid
you will be my rock
the wooden curves that feel so familiar
the feel of your neck in my hands
the tension of strings brought to one another
My soul will be lost in each and every stroke
I will run my hands down your sides
and tap your hollow belly
and find all the comfort of the deepest notes
I will allow my frame to shudder
and my bow will vibrate
like the world is falling apart beneath me
I will play you the way the first symphony ever resound in my head
you will be the first strings my fingers ever tamed
You will be the instrument I paint this world with

Take

Its losing yourself.
You just start at the tide
and slowly walk into the sea.
You can feel the lowness tremble
all around you.
The salt sweeps you clean.
It is the salt of a hundred hands
and bodies.
this is what the sea is made of.
It pulls you in.
and all you can really hope for,
is the chance that you might emerge.
Changed.
possibly for the better,
but more likely, for the worse.

Drip

Its the drip
the thing that happens when its been going too long
with too little
its when you sit down
and become a Dali painting
the time begins to melt
and youre a charcoal drawing left in a humid space
the form still remains
the stain on the paper is present
but you drip down the page
like cheap mascara on a weepy eyed girl

Dust

Then it changed
the mundane had seeped in
i was stagnant
Life became routine
because there was no one i could share it with
there was no TMNT love
but I saw a subway car spew forth
i saw you open up in a way
that i found uncomfortable
i like the way your knee feels on mine
i like the way you know art,
know it
its you
i am rarely impressed and
i was
by you
Thank you
i spent the entire evening in familiarity
in the comfort of friends
and I thought about nothing but your ears

Have Ya?

have you ever lifted her arm,
wrapped your fingers around her wrist,
and just run you hand,
down the entire length of her body?
let yourself feel the thickness of her arm,
the dimples beneath them,
each notch of her ribs,
and cupped the meat of her breasts?
Fondled the indentation right before her hips bloom,
the girth right beneath her ass,
the amazing feeling of going from hip to thigh,
the back of her calves in your hands,
and her ankles between your fingers?
well, have you?

Take Down

i want to consume you
I want to earn my namesake
I will wrap around you seamlessly
let my roots permeate your crevices
i will grow from between the cracks in your toes
and let my vines fill every wrinkle and dimple
I will wrap my limbs around you
you will be my wall
I will pull you into me
Until you have become my innards
I will slowly embrace you until we are one

Orchestra of Adoration

I can feel your fingers move across my skin
placing your fingers on the frets
playing me with the greatest of ease
i am your instrument
strings pushed and pulled
your bow bringing forth a symphony of lust
The thumping of the rhythm section echoes in my ears
the placement of your miraculous fingers on each key
You are mine
my orchestra of adoration

The Performance

I could see music
as it coursed through your veins
Melody rolling off your back
like autumn rain off a pumpkin

the joy present beneath your feet
as you walk the stage
heels heavy with soul

you did not simply play the music
but instead
took residence within
a sense of honesty
permeating the room

I could feel the sound
as it began to breathe

exist

the fingers
of each musicians soul
inexplicably intertwined
with that of the others

instruments became vessels
to a new kind of freedom

Infectious

the seduction of the nervous twitch
those things that make you too close for comfort
the things that strike my heart strings
brittle and broken
they play on
my bow is losing its hair
and my rosin is nothing but a nub
and yet i continue on, unscathed
unwilling to wander from the path into the thicket
im the weed lost among the bundle of blossoms
and i would have it no other way
dandelions have always struck my chords
short lived and infectious in nature
all that I strive for

Awe (Die Hard)

i sat down
i had my whiskey
and my fire
and all the notes I needed to bring the piece out
from deep inside of me
i had strokes that led me to figures
i felt the moment, the dance flowing up from me
I used to find these notes in you
i used find myself in you
and now that youre gone
I must bring you out
onto this canvas
bring you to life through me
we are the tunnel
it goes both ways
and always ends the same
a magnificent explosive collision
thats leaves the onlooker in awe

Once

shit
i was a writer once
i knew the nuance of the words at my finger tips
it seems things change
i now sit in solitude
dreaming of the dictionaries
and words long lost
dreams dont die
they fall away slowly
they fade and waiver
its a quiver at the tips of your fingers
its the treble in your base
they never go away
as long as there is one tiny sliver
they are yours
keep them close

ABOUT THE AUTHOR

This one time Ivy wrote something. Then she made it a book. Good times
were had by all..
Ivy Maxey Truhlar is an artist, writer, and amateur moonwalker from
Denver. Born and raised in Colorado, she graduated from the Kansas City
Art Institute, with an Emphasis in Fibers. She has done many styles of art,
from painting to felt sculpture, and some of her work has been sold and
shown in galleries. Her writing, like her artwork, is both earthy and
sensual. She currently lives in Englewood, Colorado, with a very serious
sheepdog named Gracera, and a flamboyant long-haired dachshund named
Murray.

.

15988356R00074